50 The Instant Pot Dinner Collection Recipes

By: Kelly Johnson

Table of Contents

- Beef Stroganoff
- Chicken and Rice Casserole
- Teriyaki Chicken
- Pork Carnitas
- Spaghetti Bolognese
- Chili Con Carne
- Chicken Tikka Masala
- Shrimp Scampi
- BBQ Ribs
- Beef and Broccoli
- Stuffed Bell Peppers
- Lamb Shanks
- Chicken Parmesan
- Baked Ziti
- Sweet and Sour Chicken
- Thai Red Curry Chicken
- Chicken and Dumplings
- Beef Short Ribs
- Lemon Garlic Salmon
- Pot Roast with Vegetables
- Jambalaya
- Butternut Squash Soup
- Chicken Fajitas
- Creamy Mushroom Risotto
- Beef Stew
- Eggplant Parmesan
- Chicken Enchiladas
- Tuscan Chicken
- Spicy Beef Chili
- Korean Beef Bulgogi
- Chicken Alfredo Pasta
- Meatloaf with Mashed Potatoes
- Shrimp and Grits
- Creamy Tortellini Soup
- Chicken and Sausage Gumbo

- Buffalo Chicken Wings
- Pork Shoulder Roast
- Mediterranean Chicken
- Lentil Soup
- Mexican Rice and Beans
- Turkey Meatballs in Marinara
- Stuffed Cabbage Rolls
- Chicken Sausage and Peppers
- Balsamic Glazed Pork Tenderloin
- Pasta Primavera
- Moroccan Chicken Tagine
- Beef Fajitas
- Clam Chowder
- Vegetable Soup
- Pesto Chicken

Beef Stroganoff

Ingredients:

- **1 lb beef sirloin or tenderloin**, sliced into strips
- **1 medium onion**, chopped
- **2 cloves garlic**, minced
- **8 oz mushrooms**, sliced
- **1 cup beef broth**
- **1 cup sour cream**
- **1 tablespoon Dijon mustard**
- **2 tablespoons flour**
- **2 tablespoons butter**
- **Salt and pepper**, to taste
- **Egg noodles or rice**, for serving

Instructions:

1. In a large skillet, melt butter over medium-high heat. Add the beef and season with salt and pepper. Sear the beef for about 3-4 minutes, until browned. Remove the beef and set aside.
2. In the same skillet, add the onions and garlic and sauté for 2-3 minutes, until softened. Add the mushrooms and cook for an additional 3-4 minutes until they release their juices.
3. Sprinkle the flour over the vegetables and stir well to combine. Gradually add the beef broth, stirring constantly to prevent lumps. Bring the mixture to a simmer and cook for 3-4 minutes.
4. Lower the heat and stir in the sour cream and Dijon mustard. Add the beef back to the skillet and cook for 2-3 minutes, until the sauce is heated through.
5. Serve the beef stroganoff over cooked egg noodles or rice.

Chicken and Rice Casserole

Ingredients:

- 2 cups cooked chicken, shredded
- 1 1/2 cups rice, uncooked
- 1 can cream of mushroom soup
- 1 can cream of chicken soup
- 1 cup chicken broth
- 1 cup shredded cheddar cheese
- 1/2 cup milk
- 1/2 cup frozen peas
- 1 tablespoon onion powder
- 1 tablespoon garlic powder
- Salt and pepper, to taste

Instructions:

1. Preheat the oven to 350°F (175°C).
2. In a large mixing bowl, combine the shredded chicken, rice, cream of mushroom soup, cream of chicken soup, chicken broth, milk, peas, and seasonings. Stir well to combine.
3. Pour the mixture into a greased 9x13-inch baking dish and cover with aluminum foil.
4. Bake for 45 minutes, then remove the foil and bake for an additional 10 minutes until the top is golden and the casserole is bubbly.
5. Sprinkle with shredded cheddar cheese and return to the oven for 5 minutes until the cheese is melted and bubbly.
6. Serve warm.

Teriyaki Chicken

Ingredients:

- **4 boneless, skinless chicken breasts**
- **1/2 cup soy sauce**
- **1/4 cup honey**
- **1/4 cup rice vinegar**
- **2 cloves garlic**, minced
- **1 tablespoon ginger**, grated
- **1 tablespoon sesame oil**
- **2 tablespoons cornstarch**
- **1 tablespoon water**
- **Sesame seeds and green onions**, for garnish

Instructions:

1. In a bowl, whisk together soy sauce, honey, rice vinegar, garlic, ginger, and sesame oil to create the marinade.
2. Place the chicken breasts in a resealable plastic bag or shallow dish and pour the marinade over the chicken. Marinate in the refrigerator for at least 30 minutes (or up to 4 hours).
3. Heat a grill or skillet over medium-high heat. Remove the chicken from the marinade (reserve the marinade) and cook the chicken for 6-7 minutes on each side, until cooked through.
4. In a small saucepan, bring the reserved marinade to a simmer. Mix cornstarch and water together to create a slurry, then stir it into the marinade to thicken it.
5. Drizzle the teriyaki sauce over the grilled chicken and garnish with sesame seeds and chopped green onions before serving.

Pork Carnitas

Ingredients:

- **2 lbs pork shoulder**, cut into large chunks
- **1 onion**, quartered
- **4 cloves garlic**, smashed
- **1 orange**, halved
- **2 teaspoons cumin**
- **1 teaspoon chili powder**
- **1 teaspoon oregano**
- **1 bay leaf**
- **1/2 cup chicken broth**
- **Salt and pepper**, to taste
- **Tortillas**, for serving

Instructions:

1. Place the pork shoulder chunks, onion, garlic, orange halves, cumin, chili powder, oregano, bay leaf, and chicken broth in a slow cooker.
2. Season with salt and pepper and cook on low for 8 hours, or until the pork is tender and easily shredded.
3. Remove the pork from the slow cooker and shred using two forks.
4. Heat a skillet over medium-high heat and add the shredded pork. Sauté for 5-7 minutes, allowing the edges of the pork to crisp up.
5. Serve the carnitas in tortillas with your favorite toppings such as cilantro, lime, and salsa.

Spaghetti Bolognese

Ingredients:

- **1 lb ground beef**
- **1 onion**, chopped
- **2 cloves garlic**, minced
- **1 can crushed tomatoes** (28 oz)
- **1/4 cup tomato paste**
- **1/2 cup red wine** (optional)
- **1 tablespoon dried oregano**
- **1 tablespoon dried basil**
- **1/2 teaspoon salt**
- **1/2 teaspoon pepper**
- **1 lb spaghetti**
- **Parmesan cheese**, for serving

Instructions:

1. In a large skillet, cook the ground beef over medium-high heat until browned, breaking it apart with a spoon.
2. Add the chopped onion and garlic, and sauté for 3-4 minutes until softened.
3. Stir in the crushed tomatoes, tomato paste, red wine (if using), oregano, basil, salt, and pepper. Simmer the sauce on low for 30-40 minutes, stirring occasionally.
4. Meanwhile, cook the spaghetti according to the package instructions. Drain and return to the pot.
5. Serve the Bolognese sauce over the cooked spaghetti and top with Parmesan cheese.

Chili Con Carne

Ingredients:

- **1 lb ground beef**
- **1 onion**, chopped
- **2 cloves garlic**, minced
- **1 can kidney beans** (15 oz), drained and rinsed
- **1 can diced tomatoes** (15 oz)
- **1 can tomato paste** (6 oz)
- **1 tablespoon chili powder**
- **1 teaspoon cumin**
- **1 teaspoon paprika**
- **Salt and pepper**, to taste
- **1/2 cup beef broth**

Instructions:

1. In a large pot, brown the ground beef over medium heat. Drain excess fat if needed.
2. Add the onion and garlic, and sauté for 3-4 minutes until softened.
3. Stir in the beans, diced tomatoes, tomato paste, chili powder, cumin, paprika, salt, and pepper.
4. Add beef broth and bring the mixture to a simmer. Cook for 30 minutes, stirring occasionally.
5. Serve the chili with your favorite toppings such as sour cream, cheese, or green onions.

Chicken Tikka Masala

Ingredients:

- **4 boneless, skinless chicken breasts**, cut into chunks
- **1 cup plain yogurt**
- **2 tablespoons garam masala**
- **1 tablespoon cumin**
- **1 tablespoon coriander**
- **2 tablespoons lemon juice**
- **2 tablespoons vegetable oil**
- **1 onion**, chopped
- **2 cloves garlic**, minced
- **1-inch piece ginger**, grated
- **1 can diced tomatoes** (14 oz)
- **1 cup heavy cream**
- **Fresh cilantro**, for garnish

Instructions:

1. In a bowl, mix the yogurt, garam masala, cumin, coriander, and lemon juice. Add the chicken pieces and marinate for at least 30 minutes.
2. Heat the oil in a large skillet over medium heat. Add the onion, garlic, and ginger and sauté until fragrant, about 5 minutes.
3. Add the marinated chicken to the skillet and cook for 5-7 minutes until browned.
4. Stir in the diced tomatoes and bring to a simmer. Cook for 10 minutes.
5. Add the heavy cream and cook for an additional 5 minutes. Garnish with fresh cilantro.
6. Serve with rice or naan.

Shrimp Scampi

Ingredients:

- **1 lb shrimp**, peeled and deveined
- **8 oz linguine pasta**
- **4 tablespoons butter**
- **4 cloves garlic**, minced
- **1/2 cup white wine**
- **1 tablespoon lemon juice**
- **1/4 teaspoon red pepper flakes**
- **1/4 cup fresh parsley**, chopped
- **Salt and pepper**, to taste

Instructions:

1. Cook the linguine according to package instructions. Drain and set aside, reserving 1/2 cup of pasta water.
2. In a large skillet, melt the butter over medium heat. Add the garlic and red pepper flakes and sauté for 1 minute.
3. Add the shrimp to the skillet and cook for 3-4 minutes, until pink and cooked through.
4. Pour in the white wine and lemon juice, scraping up any bits from the bottom of the skillet. Simmer for 2 minutes.
5. Add the cooked pasta to the skillet, tossing to coat. Add reserved pasta water if needed to loosen the sauce.
6. Garnish with fresh parsley and serve immediately.

BBQ Ribs

Ingredients:

- 2 racks baby back ribs
- 1/2 cup **BBQ sauce** (your choice of flavor)
- 1/4 cup brown sugar
- 1 tablespoon paprika
- 1 tablespoon garlic powder
- 1 tablespoon onion powder
- 1 teaspoon chili powder
- 1 teaspoon ground cumin
- 1 teaspoon salt
- 1 teaspoon black pepper

Instructions:

1. Preheat your oven to 300°F (150°C).
2. In a small bowl, combine brown sugar, paprika, garlic powder, onion powder, chili powder, cumin, salt, and pepper.
3. Remove the silver skin from the ribs and rub the spice mixture generously over both sides of the ribs.
4. Place the ribs on a baking sheet and cover with foil. Bake for 2.5 to 3 hours, until the ribs are tender.
5. Preheat the grill to medium heat. Remove the ribs from the oven and brush with your favorite BBQ sauce.
6. Grill the ribs for 5-10 minutes, turning occasionally and basting with more sauce until caramelized.
7. Slice and serve with extra BBQ sauce.

Beef and Broccoli

Ingredients:

- **1 lb flank steak or sirloin**, thinly sliced
- **2 cups broccoli florets**
- **1/4 cup soy sauce**
- **1/4 cup oyster sauce**
- **2 tablespoons hoisin sauce**
- **2 tablespoons cornstarch**
- **2 tablespoons water**
- **1 tablespoon sesame oil**
- **3 cloves garlic**, minced
- **1 teaspoon fresh ginger**, grated
- **1 tablespoon vegetable oil** (for stir-frying)
- **1 teaspoon sesame seeds** (optional)

Instructions:

1. In a small bowl, mix soy sauce, oyster sauce, hoisin sauce, cornstarch, and water to make the sauce. Set aside.
2. Heat vegetable oil in a large skillet over medium-high heat. Add the beef slices and stir-fry for 2-3 minutes until browned. Remove and set aside.
3. In the same skillet, add sesame oil. Sauté garlic and ginger for 1 minute until fragrant.
4. Add the broccoli and stir-fry for 4-5 minutes until bright green and tender.
5. Return the beef to the skillet and pour in the sauce. Stir to coat and cook for 2-3 minutes until the sauce thickens.
6. Serve with rice and garnish with sesame seeds.

Stuffed Bell Peppers

Ingredients:

- **4 large bell peppers**, tops cut off and seeds removed
- **1 lb ground beef** or turkey
- **1 onion**, chopped
- **2 cloves garlic**, minced
- **1 can diced tomatoes** (14.5 oz)
- **1/2 cup cooked rice**
- **1 cup shredded cheese** (cheddar or mozzarella)
- **1 tablespoon Italian seasoning**
- **Salt and pepper**, to taste

Instructions:

1. Preheat the oven to 375°F (190°C).
2. In a skillet, cook the ground meat over medium heat until browned. Add the onion and garlic, cooking for 3-4 minutes until softened.
3. Stir in the diced tomatoes, cooked rice, Italian seasoning, salt, and pepper. Simmer for 5 minutes.
4. Stuff the bell peppers with the beef and rice mixture and place them in a baking dish.
5. Cover with foil and bake for 30 minutes. Remove foil, top with cheese, and bake for an additional 10 minutes until the cheese is melted and bubbly.
6. Serve warm.

Lamb Shanks

Ingredients:

- **4 lamb shanks**
- **2 tablespoons olive oil**
- **2 onions**, chopped
- **4 cloves garlic**, minced
- **2 cups red wine**
- **1 can crushed tomatoes** (14.5 oz)
- **2 cups beef broth**
- **1 tablespoon fresh rosemary**, chopped
- **1 tablespoon thyme**
- **Salt and pepper**, to taste

Instructions:

1. Preheat the oven to 325°F (165°C).
2. Heat olive oil in a large oven-safe pot over medium-high heat. Brown the lamb shanks on all sides, about 6-8 minutes. Remove the shanks and set aside.
3. Add onions and garlic to the pot, cooking until softened, about 5 minutes.
4. Pour in the wine, scraping the bottom of the pot to release any brown bits. Add crushed tomatoes, beef broth, rosemary, thyme, salt, and pepper.
5. Return the lamb shanks to the pot and cover. Transfer the pot to the oven and braise for 2-2.5 hours, until the lamb is tender and falling off the bone.
6. Serve the lamb shanks with the sauce spooned over the top.

Chicken Parmesan

Ingredients:

- 4 boneless, skinless chicken breasts
- 1 cup breadcrumbs
- 1/2 cup grated Parmesan cheese
- **1 egg**, beaten
- 2 cups marinara sauce
- 1 1/2 cups shredded mozzarella cheese
- **1/4 cup fresh basil**, chopped
- **Olive oil**, for frying

Instructions:

1. Preheat the oven to 375°F (190°C).
2. Mix breadcrumbs and Parmesan cheese in a shallow bowl. Dip each chicken breast into the beaten egg, then coat with the breadcrumb mixture.
3. Heat olive oil in a skillet over medium heat. Cook the chicken for 4-5 minutes on each side, until golden brown. Remove and set aside.
4. In a baking dish, spread some marinara sauce, then place the chicken breasts on top. Spoon more sauce over the chicken, then top with mozzarella cheese.
5. Bake for 15-20 minutes, until the cheese is melted and bubbly.
6. Garnish with fresh basil and serve with pasta.

Baked Ziti

Ingredients:

- 1 lb ziti pasta
- 1 jar marinara sauce (24 oz)
- 1 lb ricotta cheese
- 2 cups shredded mozzarella cheese
- 1/2 cup grated Parmesan cheese
- **2 cloves garlic**, minced
- **1 tablespoon olive oil**
- **1 teaspoon dried oregano**
- **Salt and pepper**, to taste

Instructions:

1. Preheat the oven to 350°F (175°C).
2. Cook the ziti pasta according to package instructions. Drain and set aside.
3. In a large mixing bowl, combine ricotta cheese, half of the mozzarella, Parmesan cheese, garlic, oregano, salt, and pepper.
4. In a baking dish, spread a layer of marinara sauce, then add half of the cooked ziti. Top with half of the cheese mixture. Repeat with remaining pasta and cheese mixture.
5. Sprinkle the top with the remaining mozzarella cheese.
6. Bake for 25-30 minutes until the cheese is bubbly and golden. Serve warm.

Sweet and Sour Chicken

Ingredients:

- **1 lb boneless, skinless chicken breasts**, cut into cubes
- **1/2 cup flour**
- **2 eggs**, beaten
- **1/4 cup vegetable oil**
- **1 bell pepper**, chopped
- **1/2 onion**, chopped
- **1/2 cup pineapple chunks** (fresh or canned)
- **1/4 cup rice vinegar**
- **1/4 cup ketchup**
- **1/4 cup brown sugar**
- **1 tablespoon soy sauce**

Instructions:

1. Coat the chicken cubes in flour, then dip in the beaten eggs.
2. Heat vegetable oil in a skillet over medium-high heat. Cook the chicken in batches for 3-4 minutes per side, until golden brown. Remove and set aside.
3. In the same skillet, add bell pepper, onion, and pineapple chunks. Sauté for 2-3 minutes until softened.
4. In a small bowl, whisk together rice vinegar, ketchup, brown sugar, and soy sauce. Pour the sauce over the vegetables in the skillet and bring to a simmer for 2 minutes.
5. Add the chicken back to the skillet, stirring to coat in the sauce. Cook for an additional 3-4 minutes, until heated through.
6. Serve with rice.

Thai Red Curry Chicken

Ingredients:

- **1 lb chicken breasts**, cut into strips
- **1 tablespoon red curry paste**
- **1 can coconut milk** (13.5 oz)
- **1 tablespoon fish sauce**
- **1 tablespoon sugar**
- **2 cloves garlic**, minced
- **1 tablespoon ginger**, grated
- **1 bell pepper**, sliced
- **1/2 cup bamboo shoots** (optional)
- **Fresh basil**, for garnish
- **Jasmine rice**, for serving

Instructions:

1. In a large skillet, heat a tablespoon of oil over medium heat. Add chicken and cook until browned, about 6-7 minutes. Remove and set aside.
2. In the same skillet, add garlic, ginger, and red curry paste. Stir for 1 minute, then add coconut milk, fish sauce, and sugar. Bring to a simmer.
3. Add bell pepper and bamboo shoots, and cook for 4-5 minutes until tender.
4. Return the chicken to the skillet and simmer for another 5 minutes, until the chicken is fully cooked.
5. Garnish with fresh basil and serve with jasmine rice.

Chicken and Dumplings

Ingredients:

- 2 tablespoons butter
- 1 onion, chopped
- 2 carrots, chopped
- 2 celery stalks, chopped
- 3 cloves garlic, minced
- 4 cups chicken broth
- 2 cups cooked chicken, shredded
- 1 cup heavy cream
- 2 cups all-purpose flour
- 2 teaspoons baking powder
- 1 teaspoon salt
- 1/2 cup milk
- 1/4 cup chopped parsley

Instructions:

1. In a large pot, melt butter over medium heat. Add onion, carrots, celery, and garlic, cooking for 5-6 minutes until softened.
2. Add chicken broth and bring to a simmer. Stir in cooked chicken and heavy cream. Let simmer while you prepare the dumplings.
3. In a separate bowl, whisk together flour, baking powder, and salt. Stir in milk to form a dough.
4. Drop spoonfuls of dumpling dough into the simmering soup. Cover and cook for 15-20 minutes, until the dumplings are fluffy and cooked through.
5. Garnish with parsley and serve hot.

Beef Short Ribs

Ingredients:

- 4 beef short ribs
- 1 tablespoon olive oil
- **1 onion**, chopped
- **2 carrots**, peeled and chopped
- **2 celery stalks**, chopped
- **4 cloves garlic**, minced
- 2 cups red wine
- 2 cups beef broth
- 1 tablespoon tomato paste
- **2 teaspoons fresh rosemary**, chopped
- 2 teaspoons fresh thyme
- **Salt and pepper**, to taste

Instructions:

1. Preheat your oven to 325°F (165°C).
2. Heat olive oil in a large oven-safe pot over medium-high heat. Brown the short ribs on all sides, about 8-10 minutes. Remove and set aside.
3. In the same pot, add onions, carrots, and celery, cooking for 5-6 minutes until softened. Add garlic and cook for 1 more minute.
4. Stir in the tomato paste and cook for 2 minutes. Pour in the red wine, scraping up any brown bits from the bottom of the pot.
5. Add beef broth, rosemary, thyme, salt, and pepper. Return the short ribs to the pot and bring to a simmer.
6. Cover and transfer to the oven. Braise for 2.5 to 3 hours until the meat is tender and falling off the bone.
7. Serve with mashed potatoes or roasted vegetables.

Lemon Garlic Salmon

Ingredients:

- **4 salmon fillets**
- **2 tablespoons olive oil**
- **1 lemon**, sliced
- **3 cloves garlic**, minced
- **2 tablespoons fresh parsley**, chopped
- **Salt and pepper**, to taste

Instructions:

1. Preheat the oven to 375°F (190°C).
2. Place the salmon fillets on a baking sheet lined with parchment paper.
3. Drizzle with olive oil, then sprinkle with garlic, salt, and pepper. Top with lemon slices.
4. Roast for 12-15 minutes until the salmon flakes easily with a fork.
5. Garnish with fresh parsley and serve with your choice of side dish.

Pot Roast with Vegetables

Ingredients:

- 3 lb chuck roast
- 2 tablespoons olive oil
- **1 onion**, chopped
- **3 cloves garlic**, minced
- **4 carrots**, peeled and chopped
- **4 potatoes**, peeled and cubed
- 2 cups beef broth
- 1 cup red wine
- 2 teaspoons fresh thyme
- 2 bay leaves
- **Salt and pepper**, to taste

Instructions:

1. Preheat the oven to 300°F (150°C).
2. Heat olive oil in a large pot or Dutch oven over medium-high heat. Brown the roast on all sides, about 8 minutes. Remove and set aside.
3. Add onions and garlic to the pot, cooking for 3-4 minutes until softened. Stir in the carrots and potatoes.
4. Pour in beef broth and red wine, then add thyme, bay leaves, salt, and pepper.
5. Return the roast to the pot, cover, and cook in the oven for 3-4 hours, until the roast is fork-tender.
6. Slice the roast and serve with the vegetables and sauce.

Jambalaya

Ingredients:

- **1 lb chicken breast**, diced
- **1/2 lb smoked sausage**, sliced
- **1 bell pepper**, chopped
- **1 onion**, chopped
- **2 cloves garlic**, minced
- **1 can diced tomatoes** (14.5 oz)
- **1 1/2 cups long-grain rice**
- **2 cups chicken broth**
- **1 tablespoon Cajun seasoning**
- **1 teaspoon smoked paprika**
- **1/2 teaspoon thyme**
- **Salt and pepper**, to taste
- **1/2 lb shrimp**, peeled and deveined

Instructions:

1. In a large skillet, cook the chicken and sausage over medium heat until browned. Remove and set aside.
2. In the same skillet, sauté bell pepper, onion, and garlic for 5-6 minutes until softened.
3. Stir in the diced tomatoes, rice, chicken broth, Cajun seasoning, paprika, thyme, salt, and pepper. Bring to a boil.
4. Reduce heat, cover, and simmer for 15-20 minutes until the rice is cooked.
5. Add the shrimp and cooked chicken and sausage to the skillet. Cook for another 5-7 minutes until the shrimp are pink and cooked through.
6. Serve hot.

Butternut Squash Soup

Ingredients:

- **1 medium butternut squash**, peeled and cubed
- **1 onion**, chopped
- **2 cloves garlic**, minced
- **1 carrot**, peeled and chopped
- **4 cups vegetable broth**
- **1 teaspoon ground cinnamon**
- **1/2 teaspoon ground nutmeg**
- **Salt and pepper**, to taste
- **1 tablespoon olive oil**
- **1/4 cup heavy cream** (optional)

Instructions:

1. Heat olive oil in a large pot over medium heat. Add the onion, garlic, and carrot, cooking for 5-6 minutes until softened.
2. Add the cubed butternut squash, cinnamon, nutmeg, salt, and pepper. Stir to combine.
3. Pour in vegetable broth and bring to a boil. Reduce heat and simmer for 20-25 minutes, until the squash is tender.
4. Use an immersion blender to purée the soup until smooth. If you don't have an immersion blender, transfer the soup in batches to a blender.
5. Stir in heavy cream if desired and adjust seasoning. Serve hot.

Chicken Fajitas

Ingredients:

- **4 boneless, skinless chicken breasts**, thinly sliced
- **1 bell pepper**, sliced
- **1 onion**, sliced
- **2 tablespoons olive oil**
- **2 teaspoons chili powder**
- **1 teaspoon cumin**
- **1 teaspoon paprika**
- **1/2 teaspoon garlic powder**
- **1/2 teaspoon onion powder**
- **Salt and pepper**, to taste
- **Flour tortillas**, for serving
- **Sour cream, salsa, and lime wedges**, for garnish

Instructions:

1. In a bowl, combine chili powder, cumin, paprika, garlic powder, onion powder, salt, and pepper.
2. Toss the chicken with the spice mixture and olive oil. Let marinate for 15 minutes.
3. Heat a large skillet over medium-high heat. Cook the chicken for 5-6 minutes until browned and cooked through. Remove and set aside.
4. In the same skillet, sauté the bell pepper and onion for 4-5 minutes until softened.
5. Return the chicken to the skillet and toss to combine. Warm the tortillas in a dry skillet.
6. Serve the fajitas with tortillas, sour cream, salsa, and lime wedges.

Creamy Mushroom Risotto

Ingredients:

- 1 cup Arborio rice
- 2 tablespoons olive oil
- **1 small onion**, chopped
- **3 cloves garlic**, minced
- **2 cups mushrooms**, sliced
- **4 cups chicken or vegetable broth**, kept warm
- **1/2 cup white wine**
- **1/4 cup Parmesan cheese**, grated
- **Salt and pepper**, to taste

Instructions:

1. Heat olive oil in a large pan over medium heat. Add onion and garlic, cooking for 2-3 minutes until softened.
2. Add mushrooms and cook for 5-6 minutes, until browned.
3. Stir in the Arborio rice and cook for 1-2 minutes until lightly toasted.
4. Pour in white wine and cook, stirring, until absorbed.
5. Add broth, one ladle at a time, stirring constantly until the liquid is absorbed before adding more.
6. Continue until the rice is creamy and tender, about 20-25 minutes.
7. Stir in Parmesan cheese and season with salt and pepper. Serve immediately.

Beef Stew

Ingredients:

- **2 lbs beef stew meat**, cubed
- **2 tablespoons olive oil**
- **1 onion**, chopped
- **3 carrots**, peeled and chopped
- **3 potatoes**, peeled and cubed
- **3 cloves garlic**, minced
- **2 cups beef broth**
- **1 cup red wine**
- **2 teaspoons fresh thyme**
- **2 bay leaves**
- **Salt and pepper**, to taste

Instructions:

1. Heat olive oil in a large pot over medium-high heat. Brown the beef cubes in batches, then set aside.
2. Add onions and garlic to the pot, cooking for 4-5 minutes until softened. Stir in carrots and potatoes.
3. Pour in beef broth, red wine, thyme, bay leaves, salt, and pepper. Bring to a simmer.
4. Return the beef to the pot, cover, and simmer for 2-2.5 hours, until the beef is tender and the vegetables are cooked through.
5. Remove the bay leaves and serve hot.

Eggplant Parmesan

Ingredients:

- **2 medium eggplants**, sliced into 1/2-inch rounds
- **2 cups marinara sauce**
- **1 1/2 cups mozzarella cheese**, shredded
- **1/2 cup Parmesan cheese**, grated
- **1 cup breadcrumbs**
- **1/2 cup flour**
- **2 eggs**, beaten
- **Olive oil**, for frying
- **Fresh basil**, for garnish

Instructions:

1. Preheat the oven to 375°F (190°C).
2. Dredge eggplant slices in flour, dip in beaten eggs, then coat in breadcrumbs.
3. Heat olive oil in a skillet over medium-high heat. Fry eggplant slices in batches for 2-3 minutes per side, until golden brown.
4. In a baking dish, layer fried eggplant slices with marinara sauce and mozzarella cheese.
5. Top with Parmesan cheese and bake for 25-30 minutes until the cheese is bubbly and golden.
6. Garnish with fresh basil and serve.

Chicken Enchiladas

Ingredients:

- **2 cups cooked chicken**, shredded
- **2 cups enchilada sauce**
- **8 flour tortillas**
- **1 cup cheddar cheese**, shredded
- **1 cup sour cream**
- **1/2 onion**, chopped
- **1 tablespoon olive oil**

Instructions:

1. Preheat the oven to 350°F (175°C).
2. Heat olive oil in a pan and sauté the onion for 4-5 minutes until softened.
3. Add the shredded chicken and 1 cup of enchilada sauce. Stir to combine.
4. Fill tortillas with the chicken mixture, roll them up, and place them in a baking dish.
5. Pour the remaining enchilada sauce over the rolled tortillas and sprinkle with cheese.
6. Bake for 20-25 minutes, until the cheese is melted and bubbly.
7. Serve with sour cream and garnish with chopped cilantro.

Tuscan Chicken

Ingredients:

- 4 boneless, skinless chicken breasts
- 2 tablespoons olive oil
- 1 teaspoon dried oregano
- 1 teaspoon dried basil
- 1/2 teaspoon garlic powder
- **Salt and pepper**, to taste
- 1 cup **sun-dried tomatoes**, chopped
- 1/2 cup **heavy cream**
- 1/2 cup **chicken broth**
- 1 cup **spinach**, fresh
- 1/2 cup **Parmesan cheese**, grated

Instructions:

1. Season chicken breasts with oregano, basil, garlic powder, salt, and pepper.
2. Heat olive oil in a large skillet over medium-high heat. Cook chicken breasts for 6-7 minutes on each side until golden brown and cooked through. Remove from the skillet and set aside.
3. In the same skillet, add sun-dried tomatoes, heavy cream, chicken broth, and spinach. Stir and cook for 3-4 minutes until the spinach wilts and the sauce thickens.
4. Return the chicken to the skillet and simmer for an additional 5-6 minutes. Sprinkle with Parmesan cheese before serving.

Spicy Beef Chili

Ingredients:

- 1 lb ground beef
- **1 onion**, chopped
- **2 cloves garlic**, minced
- **2 tablespoons chili powder**
- **1 teaspoon cumin**
- **1 teaspoon paprika**
- **1 can diced tomatoes** (14.5 oz)
- **1 can kidney beans**, drained and rinsed
- **1 can black beans**, drained and rinsed
- **1 can green chilies** (4 oz)
- **1/2 cup beef broth**
- **Salt and pepper**, to taste
- **Hot sauce**, to taste (optional)

Instructions:

1. In a large pot, brown the ground beef over medium heat, breaking it up as it cooks. Drain excess fat.
2. Add chopped onion and garlic, and cook for 3-4 minutes until softened.
3. Stir in chili powder, cumin, paprika, salt, and pepper. Cook for 1-2 minutes to bring out the flavors.
4. Add diced tomatoes, kidney beans, black beans, green chilies, and beef broth. Bring to a boil.
5. Reduce heat and simmer for 20-25 minutes. Taste and adjust seasoning with hot sauce or more chili powder if desired. Serve hot.

Korean Beef Bulgogi

Ingredients:

- **1 lb flank steak**, thinly sliced
- **1/4 cup soy sauce**
- **2 tablespoons brown sugar**
- **2 tablespoons sesame oil**
- **2 tablespoons rice vinegar**
- **3 cloves garlic**, minced
- **1 tablespoon fresh ginger**, grated
- **1/2 teaspoon red pepper flakes** (optional)
- **2 green onions**, chopped
- **Sesame seeds**, for garnish

Instructions:

1. In a bowl, combine soy sauce, brown sugar, sesame oil, rice vinegar, garlic, ginger, and red pepper flakes. Stir to dissolve the sugar.
2. Add the sliced beef to the marinade, cover, and refrigerate for at least 1 hour (or overnight for more flavor).
3. Heat a grill or skillet over medium-high heat. Cook the marinated beef for 3-4 minutes, stirring occasionally until browned and cooked through.
4. Garnish with green onions and sesame seeds. Serve with steamed rice or vegetables.

Chicken Alfredo Pasta

Ingredients:

- **2 boneless, skinless chicken breasts**, sliced
- **8 oz fettuccine pasta**
- **2 tablespoons butter**
- **2 cloves garlic**, minced
- **1 cup heavy cream**
- **1 cup Parmesan cheese**, grated
- **Salt and pepper**, to taste
- **Fresh parsley**, chopped, for garnish

Instructions:

1. Cook fettuccine pasta according to package directions. Drain and set aside.
2. In a skillet, melt butter over medium heat. Add the sliced chicken and cook until browned and cooked through, about 7-8 minutes.
3. Add minced garlic and cook for 1 minute until fragrant.
4. Pour in the heavy cream and bring to a simmer. Stir in Parmesan cheese and cook for 2-3 minutes until the sauce thickens.
5. Toss the cooked pasta into the skillet with the sauce. Season with salt and pepper.
6. Garnish with fresh parsley and serve.

Meatloaf with Mashed Potatoes

Ingredients for Meatloaf:

- 1 lb ground beef
- 1/2 lb ground pork
- 1 onion, chopped
- 1/2 cup breadcrumbs
- 1/4 cup milk
- 1 egg
- 1 tablespoon Worcestershire sauce
- 1 teaspoon dried thyme
- Salt and pepper, to taste
- 1/2 cup ketchup

Ingredients for Mashed Potatoes:

- 4 large potatoes, peeled and chopped
- 1/4 cup butter
- 1/2 cup milk
- Salt and pepper, to taste

Instructions:

1. Preheat the oven to 350°F (175°C).
2. In a bowl, combine ground beef, ground pork, onion, breadcrumbs, milk, egg, Worcestershire sauce, thyme, salt, and pepper. Mix well.
3. Form the meat mixture into a loaf shape and place in a baking dish. Spread ketchup over the top.
4. Bake for 1 hour or until cooked through.
5. While the meatloaf bakes, make the mashed potatoes. Boil potatoes in salted water until tender, about 15-20 minutes. Drain and return to the pot.
6. Mash potatoes with butter and milk, seasoning with salt and pepper to taste. Serve the meatloaf with mashed potatoes.

Shrimp and Grits

Ingredients:

- **1 lb shrimp**, peeled and deveined
- **2 tablespoons butter**
- **2 cloves garlic**, minced
- **1/2 teaspoon smoked paprika**
- **1/2 cup chicken broth**
- **1 cup grits**
- **4 cups water**
- **1/2 cup heavy cream**
- **1/2 cup cheddar cheese**, shredded
- **Salt and pepper**, to taste

Instructions:

1. In a medium saucepan, bring water to a boil. Add grits and cook according to package directions.
2. Stir in heavy cream and cheddar cheese once the grits are done. Keep warm.
3. In a skillet, melt butter over medium heat. Add garlic and cook for 1 minute.
4. Add shrimp to the skillet, sprinkle with smoked paprika, salt, and pepper. Cook for 3-4 minutes until shrimp turn pink.
5. Pour in chicken broth and simmer for 2-3 minutes.
6. Serve the shrimp over the cheesy grits.

Creamy Tortellini Soup

Ingredients:

- 1 lb cheese tortellini
- 1 tablespoon olive oil
- **1 onion**, chopped
- **2 cloves garlic**, minced
- **4 cups vegetable broth**
- **1 can diced tomatoes** (14.5 oz)
- **1 cup heavy cream**
- **2 cups spinach**, fresh
- **Salt and pepper**, to taste
- **Parmesan cheese**, for garnish

Instructions:

1. Cook tortellini according to package directions. Drain and set aside.
2. In a large pot, heat olive oil over medium heat. Sauté onion and garlic for 4-5 minutes until softened.
3. Add vegetable broth, diced tomatoes, and heavy cream. Bring to a simmer.
4. Stir in cooked tortellini and spinach. Cook for 3-4 minutes until spinach wilts.
5. Season with salt and pepper. Serve with a sprinkle of Parmesan cheese.

Chicken and Sausage Gumbo

Ingredients:

- **1 lb chicken thighs**, boneless and skinless, diced
- **1/2 lb sausage**, sliced (preferably andouille)
- **1 onion**, chopped
- **1 bell pepper**, chopped
- **2 celery stalks**, chopped
- **4 cups chicken broth**
- **1 can diced tomatoes** (14.5 oz)
- **2 cloves garlic**, minced
- **1 tablespoon Cajun seasoning**
- **1 teaspoon thyme**
- **Salt and pepper**, to taste
- **1/4 cup flour**
- **1/4 cup vegetable oil**
- **Rice**, for serving

Instructions:

1. In a large pot, heat oil over medium heat. Add flour and cook, whisking constantly, for about 5 minutes to make a roux.
2. Stir in onion, bell pepper, celery, and garlic. Cook for 5-6 minutes until softened.
3. Add chicken, sausage, Cajun seasoning, thyme, chicken broth, diced tomatoes, salt, and pepper. Bring to a boil.
4. Reduce heat and simmer for 45 minutes to 1 hour. Serve over rice.

Buffalo Chicken Wings

Ingredients:

- 10 chicken wings
- 1/4 cup hot sauce
- 2 tablespoons **butter**, melted
- 1 tablespoon vinegar
- 1/4 teaspoon garlic powder
- **Salt**, to taste

Instructions:

1. Preheat the oven to 400°F (200°C).
2. Arrange chicken wings on a baking sheet. Season with salt and bake for 25-30 minutes until crispy.
3. In a bowl, combine hot sauce, butter, vinegar, and garlic powder.
4. Toss the cooked wings in the sauce and serve with ranch or blue cheese dressing.

Pork Shoulder Roast

Ingredients:

- 3-4 lb pork shoulder
- 2 tablespoons olive oil
- 3 cloves garlic, minced
- 1 tablespoon thyme
- 1 tablespoon rosemary
- 1 cup chicken broth
- Salt and pepper, to taste

Instructions:

1. Preheat the oven to 350°F (175°C).
2. Rub the pork shoulder with olive oil, garlic, thyme, rosemary, salt, and pepper.
3. Roast for 3-4 hours, basting occasionally with chicken broth.
4. Remove from the oven and let rest for 10 minutes before slicing.

Mediterranean Chicken

Ingredients:

- 4 boneless, skinless chicken breasts
- 2 tablespoons olive oil
- 1 teaspoon dried oregano
- 1 teaspoon garlic powder
- **Salt and pepper**, to taste
- 1/2 cup **Kalamata olives**, pitted and chopped
- 1/2 cup **feta cheese**, crumbled
- 1/2 cup **sun-dried tomatoes**, chopped
- 1/4 cup **fresh parsley**, chopped
- 1/2 cup **lemon juice**
- 1 tablespoon olive oil (for sauce)

Instructions:

1. Preheat oven to 375°F (190°C).
2. Rub chicken breasts with olive oil, oregano, garlic powder, salt, and pepper.
3. Heat a skillet over medium-high heat, then sear chicken breasts for 2-3 minutes on each side until golden.
4. Transfer chicken to a baking dish and top with olives, feta, sun-dried tomatoes, and parsley.
5. Drizzle with lemon juice and a tablespoon of olive oil.
6. Bake for 25-30 minutes until the chicken is cooked through.
7. Serve with rice or a Mediterranean salad.

Lentil Soup

Ingredients:

- **1 cup dried lentils**, rinsed
- **1 onion**, chopped
- **2 carrots**, peeled and chopped
- **2 celery stalks**, chopped
- **3 cloves garlic**, minced
- **1 can diced tomatoes** (14.5 oz)
- **4 cups vegetable broth**
- **1 teaspoon ground cumin**
- **1/2 teaspoon turmeric**
- **Salt and pepper**, to taste
- **2 tablespoons olive oil**
- **1/4 cup fresh parsley**, chopped

Instructions:

1. Heat olive oil in a large pot over medium heat. Add onion, carrots, and celery, and cook for 5-6 minutes until softened.
2. Add garlic, cumin, and turmeric, and cook for another minute until fragrant.
3. Stir in the lentils, diced tomatoes, vegetable broth, salt, and pepper. Bring to a boil.
4. Reduce heat, cover, and simmer for 30-40 minutes, until lentils are tender.
5. Adjust seasoning if necessary and serve hot, garnished with fresh parsley.

Mexican Rice and Beans

Ingredients:

- **1 cup long-grain rice**
- **1 tablespoon olive oil**
- **1/2 onion**, chopped
- **1 can black beans** (15 oz), drained and rinsed
- **1 can diced tomatoes** (14.5 oz)
- **2 cups vegetable broth**
- **1 teaspoon cumin**
- **1 teaspoon chili powder**
- **Salt and pepper**, to taste
- **1/4 cup cilantro**, chopped

Instructions:

1. In a large skillet, heat olive oil over medium heat. Add the onion and cook for 3-4 minutes until softened.
2. Stir in rice and cook for 2 minutes, allowing it to lightly toast.
3. Add black beans, diced tomatoes, vegetable broth, cumin, chili powder, salt, and pepper.
4. Bring to a boil, then reduce heat, cover, and simmer for 20-25 minutes, until the rice is tender and the liquid is absorbed.
5. Remove from heat and fluff with a fork. Stir in chopped cilantro before serving.

Turkey Meatballs in Marinara

Ingredients for Meatballs:

- **1 lb ground turkey**
- **1/4 cup breadcrumbs**
- **1/4 cup Parmesan cheese**, grated
- **1 egg**
- **1 tablespoon dried oregano**
- **1 teaspoon garlic powder**
- **Salt and pepper**, to taste

Ingredients for Sauce:

- **1 jar marinara sauce** (24 oz)
- **1/2 teaspoon dried basil**
- **1/2 teaspoon red pepper flakes** (optional)

Instructions:

1. Preheat oven to 375°F (190°C).
2. In a large bowl, combine ground turkey, breadcrumbs, Parmesan cheese, egg, oregano, garlic powder, salt, and pepper. Mix until well combined.
3. Form into 12 meatballs and place on a baking sheet lined with parchment paper.
4. Bake for 20 minutes until cooked through.
5. While meatballs bake, heat marinara sauce in a pot over medium heat. Add basil and red pepper flakes.
6. Add baked meatballs to the sauce and simmer for 10-15 minutes.
7. Serve the meatballs in marinara sauce with pasta or crusty bread.

Stuffed Cabbage Rolls

Ingredients:

- 1 head green cabbage
- 1 lb ground beef
- 1/2 cup cooked rice
- **1 onion**, chopped
- 1 egg
- 1 teaspoon garlic powder
- 1 teaspoon dried thyme
- **1 can diced tomatoes** (14.5 oz)
- 1 cup tomato sauce
- 1 tablespoon brown sugar
- **Salt and pepper**, to taste

Instructions:

1. Bring a large pot of water to a boil. Core the cabbage and carefully remove the leaves. Boil the leaves for 2-3 minutes until softened, then set aside to cool.
2. In a bowl, combine ground beef, cooked rice, onion, egg, garlic powder, thyme, salt, and pepper.
3. Place a spoonful of the beef mixture in the center of each cabbage leaf. Roll up the leaf, folding in the sides as you go.
4. In a baking dish, layer the stuffed cabbage rolls.
5. In a separate bowl, mix diced tomatoes, tomato sauce, brown sugar, salt, and pepper. Pour over the cabbage rolls.
6. Cover the dish with foil and bake at 350°F (175°C) for 1 hour.
7. Serve hot with crusty bread.

Chicken Sausage and Peppers

Ingredients:

- **4 chicken sausages**, sliced
- **2 bell peppers**, sliced
- **1 onion**, sliced
- **2 cloves garlic**, minced
- **2 tablespoons olive oil**
- **1 teaspoon dried oregano**
- **Salt and pepper**, to taste
- **Fresh parsley**, for garnish

Instructions:

1. Heat olive oil in a large skillet over medium heat. Add chicken sausage slices and cook until browned, about 5-7 minutes.
2. Add sliced bell peppers, onion, and garlic to the skillet. Cook for 5-6 minutes, stirring occasionally, until vegetables are tender.
3. Sprinkle with oregano, salt, and pepper.
4. Serve with rice or on a bun as a sandwich, garnished with fresh parsley.

Balsamic Glazed Pork Tenderloin

Ingredients:

- **1 pork tenderloin** (about 1 lb)
- **1/4 cup balsamic vinegar**
- **1/4 cup honey**
- **2 tablespoons olive oil**
- **2 cloves garlic**, minced
- **1 teaspoon dried thyme**
- **Salt and pepper**, to taste

Instructions:

1. Preheat oven to 400°F (200°C).
2. In a small saucepan, combine balsamic vinegar, honey, olive oil, garlic, and thyme. Bring to a simmer and cook for 5-7 minutes until the glaze thickens.
3. Season pork tenderloin with salt and pepper. Heat olive oil in a skillet over medium-high heat and sear the pork for 2-3 minutes on each side.
4. Transfer the pork to a baking dish and brush with the balsamic glaze.
5. Roast for 20-25 minutes, or until the pork reaches an internal temperature of 145°F (63°C).
6. Let the pork rest for 5 minutes before slicing. Drizzle with extra glaze before serving.

Pasta Primavera

Ingredients:

- **12 oz pasta** (penne, spaghetti, or fettuccine)
- **2 tablespoons olive oil**
- **1 cup cherry tomatoes**, halved
- **1 zucchini**, sliced
- **1 bell pepper**, sliced
- **1/2 cup peas**
- **2 cloves garlic**, minced
- **1/4 cup grated Parmesan cheese**
- **1/4 cup fresh basil**, chopped
- **Salt and pepper**, to taste
- **1 tablespoon lemon juice**

Instructions:

1. Cook the pasta according to package instructions, then drain and set aside.
2. In a large skillet, heat olive oil over medium heat. Add the garlic and sauté for 1 minute.
3. Add the zucchini, bell pepper, peas, and tomatoes, and cook for 5-7 minutes until vegetables are tender.
4. Stir in the cooked pasta, Parmesan cheese, and lemon juice. Season with salt and pepper.
5. Garnish with fresh basil and serve immediately.

Moroccan Chicken Tagine

Ingredients:

- 4 bone-in, skinless chicken thighs
- 1 tablespoon olive oil
- **1 onion**, chopped
- **2 cloves garlic**, minced
- **1 tablespoon ground cumin**
- **1 teaspoon ground cinnamon**
- **1 teaspoon turmeric**
- **1 teaspoon ground ginger**
- **1/2 teaspoon paprika**
- **1 can diced tomatoes** (14.5 oz)
- **1 cup chicken broth**
- **1/2 cup dried apricots**, chopped
- **1/4 cup slivered almonds**
- **Salt and pepper**, to taste
- **Fresh cilantro**, for garnish

Instructions:

1. Heat olive oil in a tagine or large pot over medium-high heat. Season the chicken thighs with salt and pepper, and brown them on both sides, about 4-5 minutes per side. Remove from the pot and set aside.
2. In the same pot, add onion and garlic, cooking until softened, about 5 minutes.
3. Stir in the spices (cumin, cinnamon, turmeric, ginger, paprika) and cook for 1 minute until fragrant.
4. Add diced tomatoes, chicken broth, apricots, and almonds. Return the chicken to the pot.
5. Cover and simmer for 30-40 minutes, until the chicken is cooked through and tender.
6. Garnish with fresh cilantro and serve with couscous or rice.

Beef Fajitas

Ingredients:

- **1 lb flank steak** (or skirt steak)
- **1 tablespoon olive oil**
- **1 onion**, sliced
- **2 bell peppers**, sliced
- **2 cloves garlic**, minced
- **1 teaspoon ground cumin**
- **1 teaspoon chili powder**
- **1/2 teaspoon paprika**
- **1/2 teaspoon cayenne pepper** (optional)
- **Juice of 1 lime**
- **Salt and pepper**, to taste
- **Flour tortillas**, for serving
- **Sour cream**, salsa, and guacamole, for garnish

Instructions:

1. In a small bowl, mix cumin, chili powder, paprika, cayenne pepper (if using), salt, and pepper. Rub the spice mixture onto both sides of the flank steak.
2. Heat olive oil in a skillet over medium-high heat. Cook the steak for 4-5 minutes per side for medium-rare, or longer for desired doneness. Remove from the skillet and let rest.
3. In the same skillet, add onion, bell peppers, and garlic. Cook for 5-6 minutes, until vegetables are tender.
4. Slice the steak thinly against the grain and return to the skillet, tossing with the vegetables and lime juice.
5. Serve the beef and vegetable mixture in flour tortillas with sour cream, salsa, and guacamole.

Clam Chowder

Ingredients:

- **2 tablespoons butter**
- **1 onion**, chopped
- **2 stalks celery**, chopped
- **2 cloves garlic**, minced
- **2 cups potatoes**, diced
- **1 1/2 cups clam broth**
- **2 cups heavy cream**
- **1 can clams** (6.5 oz), drained and chopped
- **1 teaspoon dried thyme**
- **1/2 teaspoon salt**
- **1/4 teaspoon black pepper**
- **Fresh parsley**, for garnish

Instructions:

1. In a large pot, melt butter over medium heat. Add the onion, celery, and garlic, cooking for 5-6 minutes until softened.
2. Stir in the potatoes, clam broth, and thyme. Bring to a boil, then reduce heat and simmer for 10-15 minutes until potatoes are tender.
3. Add the heavy cream, clams, salt, and pepper, stirring well. Simmer for another 5-10 minutes to heat through.
4. Serve the chowder hot, garnished with fresh parsley.

Vegetable Soup

Ingredients:

- 2 tablespoons olive oil
- 1 onion, chopped
- 2 carrots, sliced
- 2 celery stalks, chopped
- 2 cloves garlic, minced
- 1 zucchini, chopped
- 1 cup green beans, chopped
- 1 can diced tomatoes (14.5 oz)
- 4 cups vegetable broth
- 1 teaspoon dried basil
- 1 teaspoon dried oregano
- Salt and pepper, to taste
- 1/4 cup fresh parsley, chopped

Instructions:

1. Heat olive oil in a large pot over medium heat. Add onion, carrots, and celery, and cook for 5-6 minutes until softened.
2. Add garlic and cook for 1 more minute, until fragrant.
3. Stir in zucchini, green beans, diced tomatoes, vegetable broth, basil, oregano, salt, and pepper. Bring to a boil.
4. Reduce heat and simmer for 20-25 minutes until vegetables are tender.
5. Garnish with fresh parsley and serve hot.

Pesto Chicken

Ingredients:

- 4 boneless, skinless chicken breasts
- **1/4 cup pesto sauce** (store-bought or homemade)
- **2 tablespoons olive oil**
- **1 teaspoon garlic powder**
- **Salt and pepper**, to taste
- **1/4 cup grated Parmesan cheese**

Instructions:

1. Preheat the oven to 375°F (190°C).
2. Rub the chicken breasts with olive oil, garlic powder, salt, and pepper.
3. Spread pesto sauce over the top of each chicken breast.
4. Place the chicken on a baking sheet and sprinkle with Parmesan cheese.
5. Bake for 25-30 minutes, or until the chicken reaches an internal temperature of 165°F (74°C).
6. Serve with pasta, rice, or a fresh salad.